_____

To

_____

From

We dedicate this book to our mothers and all
those who have been a mother to a child in need.
May these words and Scriptures reward, inspire,
and challenge you to carry on, knowing that
there is One who knows what you do in secret.

RON & CAESAR

THE HEART

OF A

Mother

By Ron DiCianni

COMPILED BY CAESAR KALINOWSKI

Tyndale House Publishers
WHEATON, ILLINOIS

Teach them to Pray

❦

"The best teaching our children will receive
concerning prayer will be seen with their eyes,
not heard with their ears."

Ron DiCianni

There is no higher height to which humanity can attain than that occupied by a devoted, heaven-inspired, praying mother.

—Anonymous

⚬⋀⚬

Give your children to God.
Give your own self to God.
Pray together with your children in honest terms
that are appropriate to their age and understanding.
Then daily trust God to do his work in all of you.

—Carole Sanderson Streeter

*As for me and my household,
we will serve the Lord.*

—Joshua 24:15, niv

If you must sacrifice somewhere, let it be in simpler meals, clothes, and yes, even in frequency of cleaning, if you must, but don't neglect your loved ones' souls and minds and habits. That means prayer must be a priority for the family, not an afterthought.

—FAMILY LIFE

In my opinion, what we need to teach children is that prayer is friendly conversation, frequently conversing alone, with One whom we know loves us.

—TERESA OF AVILA

[*God*] . . . is able to do immeasurably more than all we ask or imagine, according to his power that is at work within us.

—EPHESIANS 3:20, NIV

PRAY

For where two or three are gathered together
in my name, there am I in the midst of them.

—Matthew 18:20, kjv

WATCH

I will instruct you and teach you in the way
you should go; I will counsel you
and watch over you.

—Psalm 32:8, niv

WAIT

In the morning, O Lord, you hear my voice;
in the morning I lay my requests before you
and wait in expectation.

—Psalm 5:3, niv

Whether you are five, fifteen, or fifty, hearing about the details of the day you were born is always fascinating. So explain to your children how they have inherited distinct characteristics and features from each of you. The more they have a sense of their heritage, the more connected they will feel to the family and its truth standards, and the more they will want to establish a pattern of communicating with God, their Creator.

—JOSH MCDOWELL

The Golden Rule of Motherhood is:
"Tell me, and I'll forget.
Show me, and I may remember.
Involve me, and I will understand."
And that goes for your prayer life, too.
If you're not on your knees,
how could you expect your child to be?

—ANNE GRAHAM LOTZ

❦

Children of the heavenly King,
As we journey let us sing;
Sing our Savior's worthy praise,
Glorious in His works and ways.

—JOHN CENNICK

Guide me in your truth and teach me, for you are God my Savior,
and my hope is in you all day long.

—PSALM 25:5, NIV

The only way a parent can ever hope to teach the sovereignty and lordship of God—the only way a parent can teach children to love God with all their passion and commitment, with all their being and intellect, with all their energy and stamina—is for that truth to come from what the parent truly is in his or her own heart. Only when parents truly love God can his lordship express itself in what they do with their hands, in how they see things, and in the atmosphere of the home from the minute a child comes through the doorposts of the house.

—GLORIA GAITHER

O God of our Lord Jesus Christ, give my child the Spirit of wisdom and revelation so that she may know You better. Enlighten the eyes of her heart in order that she may know the hope to which You have called her, the riches of Your glorious inheritance in the saints, and Your incomparably great power for her because she believes. Help her to realize that that power is like the working of Your mighty strength, which You exerted in Christ when you raised Him from the dead. In Jesus' name, amen.

—SARAH MADDOX AND PATTI WEBB

Praise him, all you people of the earth.
For he loves us with unfailing love;
the faithfulness of the Lord endures forever.

—Psalm 117:12, nlt

❧

How important it is to teach children
not only to present their requests to God,
but also to thank and praise him for who he is and
for all his answers! By doing so, you are cultivating
a grateful heart—one that will more likely be open
to a relationship with the Father.

—Annie Daton

❧

All glory, laud, and honor
To Thee, Redeemer, King,
To whom the lips of children
Made sweet hosannas ring.

—Theodulf of Orléans

My Dear Child

I can teach you things, *but I cannot make you learn.*

I can give you directions, *but I cannot be there to lead.*

I can allow you freedom, *but I cannot account for it.*

I can take you to church, *but I cannot make you believe.*

I can teach you right from wrong, *but I cannot always decide for you.*

I can buy you beautiful clothes, *but I cannot make you beautiful inside.*

I can offer you advice, *but I cannot accept it for you.*

I can give you love, *but I cannot force it upon you.*

I can teach you to respect, *but I cannot force you to show honor.*

I can advise you about friends, *but I cannot choose them for you.*

I can advise you about sex, *but I cannot keep you pure.*

I can tell you about the facts of life, *but I cannot build your reputation.*

I can tell you about drink, *but I can't say "no" for you.*

I can warn you about drugs, *but I can't prevent you from using them.*

I can tell you about lofty goals, *but I can't achieve them for you.*

I can teach you about kindness, *but I can't force you to be gracious.*

I can warn you about sins, *but I cannot make you moral.*

I can love you as a child, *but I cannot place you in God's family.*

I can pray for you, *but I cannot make you walk with God.*

I can teach you about Jesus, *but I cannot make Jesus your Lord.*

I can tell you how to live, *but I cannot give you eternal life.*

I can love you unconditionally all my life, *and I will.*

Always, Mom

—AUTHOR UNKNOWN
Touched by an E-mail
EDITED BY DENNY MOG

$\mathcal{A}$ good rule for training children, as for anything else, is: "Pray and Labor."

—Unknown

❧

$\mathcal{A}$nd I pray that you, being rooted and established in love, may have power, together with all the saints, to grasp how wide and long and high and deep is the love of Christ, and to know this love that surpasses knowledge—that you may be filled to the measure of all the fullness of God.

—Ephesians 3:17-19, niv

❧

$\mathcal{D}$iscipline your children, and they will give you happiness and peace of mind.

—Proverbs 29:17, nlt

God's Protection

❧

"There is not a weapon on earth or hell that can penetrate the mighty hedge of protection God builds around his children."

Ron DiCianni

When you feel alone and afraid, remember who accompanies you! Turn to God for the comfort of His presence and the calming of your fears. He will embrace you as a friend with His Word. God will protect you— He is behind, alongside, and ahead of you.

—Susan Miller

❧

O God, our help in ages past,
Our hope for years to come,
Our shelter from the stormy blast,
And our eternal home!

—Isaac Watts

❧

"Do not fear, for I am with you; do not anxiously look about you, for I am your God. I will strengthen you, surely I will help you."

—Isaiah 41:10, nasb

Have you been propping up that foolish soul of yours with the idea that your circumstances are too much for God to handle? Set all your opinions and speculations aside and "abide under the shadow of the Almighty" (Psalm 91:1). Deliberately tell God that you will not fret about whatever concerns you. All our fretting and worrying is caused by planning without God.

—OSWALD CHAMBERS

There is no moment when his eye is off me, or his attention is distracted from me, no moment therefore, when his care falters. I never go unnoticed. Every moment of life is spent in the sight and company of an omniscient, omnipresent Creator.

—J. I. PACKER

I have a protection from the storm,
A shadow from the fainting heat,
I have access unto his throne,
Who is a God so wondrously great.

—ANNE BRADSTREET

✦

My times are in the hands of the Sovereign God
Whose power is limitless
And whose love for me
Is from everlasting to everlasting!

—RUTH HARMS CALKIN

✦

Just as the mountains surround and protect
Jerusalem, so the Lord surrounds and protects his
people, both now and forever.

—PSALM 125:2, NLT

The Lord is faithful, and he will strengthen and protect you from the evil one.

— 2 Thessalonians 3:3, NIV

When my time came to let go of our children, I was able to do so largely because my mother had taught me that you don't let go of a relationship—only your dependence on it. She had done it well, trusting God to protect her kids, and for this and all the other things she and Dad did, I give thanks to God. For I had a model of what to do in my own parenting.

—Jill Briscoe

The Light of God surrounds me.
The Love of God enfolds me.
The Power of God protects me.
The Presence of God watches over me.
Wherever I am, God is.

—Catherine Marshall

"Because

We may be called to go through many trials and dangers; but the protecting hand of the Lord will always be extended to us. And we shall have the peace that passeth all understanding, along with the promise of Proverbs 3:26: "For the Lord shall be thy confidence, and shall keep thy foot from being taken."

—JAMES STEWART THOMAS

Let all who take refuge in you be glad; let them ever sing for joy. Spread your protection over them, that those who love your name may rejoice in you.

—PSALM 5:11, NIV

Safety does not depend on our conception of the
absence of danger. Safety is found in God's
presence, in the center of His perfect will.

—T. J. Bach

✦

God's sovereign care assures us that nothing can
touch us until he is through with us. God is good.
God is our Hope, our Refuge.

—Ann Kiemel Anderson

✦

"Because he loves me," says the LORD,
"I will rescue him; I will protect him, for he
acknowledges my name."

—Psalm 91:14, NIV

May the strength of God pilot us.
May the power of God preserve us.
May the wisdom of God instruct us.
May the hand of God protect us.
May the way of God direct us.

—PATRICK OF IRELAND

Find rest, O my soul, in God alone; my hope comes from him. He alone is my rock and my salvation; he is my fortress, I will not be shaken. My salvation and my honor depend on God; he is my mighty rock, my refuge. Trust in him at all times, O people; pour out your hearts to him, for God is our refuge.

—PSALM 62:5-8, NIV

*I*f my trust in the fortress of the Lord is absolute, I am abiding in that fortress.

The practical thing to do since God is our Fortress and our High Tower is to surrender by faith to put ourselves and all our interests into this divine dwelling place. Then we must dismiss all care or anxiety from our minds. Since the Lord is our dwelling place, nothing can possibly come to any harm that is committed to His care.

As long as we believe this, our affairs remain in His hands. The moment we begin to doubt, we take our affairs into our own hands, and they are no longer in the divine fortress. Things cannot be in two places at once. If they are in our own care, they cannot be in God's care. And if they are in God's care, they cannot be in our own.

—HANNAH WHITALL SMITH

*T*hose who trust in the Lord are like Mount Zion,
which cannot be shaken but endures forever.

—PSALM 125:1, NIV

❧

*G*od is in control. He is never surprised by events that
surprise us. Neither is He worried over world conditions.
We rest in Him who is Lord of all. His grace, mercy,
and loving-kindness overwhelm us.

—LESLIE B. FLYNN

❧

*F*or I am persuaded, that neither death, nor life, nor angels,
nor principalities, nor powers, nor things present,
nor things to come, nor height, nor depth, nor any other
creature, shall be able to separate us from the love of God,
which is in Christ Jesus our Lord.

—ROMANS 8:38-39, KJV

ℱAITH...NOT FEAR

❧

"It is impossible to trust and worry at the same time.
A decision to trust will ultimately lead to peace.
A decision to worry will ultimately lead to needless anxiety."

Ron DiCianni

Faith is a risky business, filled challenges and experiences—

—Harriet Crosby

Day by day and with each passing moment,
  Strength I find to meet my trials here;
Trusting in my Father's wise bestowment,
  I've no cause for worry or for fear.

—Carolina Sandell Berg

Lead on, O King eternal,
  We follow, not with fears,
For gladness breaks like morning
  Where'er Thy face appears.

—Ernest Warburton Shurtleff

with trial and error, unknown and unimaginable rewards.

Faith links us to the almighty power of God, and makes it possible for our weakness to draw down unfailing supplies of His strength, poured on us out of His love.

—Hannah Whitall Smith

"Be strong and courageous! Do not tremble or be dismayed, for the Lord your God is with you wherever you go."

—Joshua 1:9, nasb

The Lord is my rock, and my fortress, and my deliverer; my God, my strength, in whom I will trust.

—Psalm 18:2, kjv

True faith depends not upon mysterious signs,
celestial fireworks, or grandiose dispensations from a God
who is seen as a rich, benevolent uncle; true faith . . .
rests on the assurance that God is who He is. Indeed,
on that we must be willing to stake our very lives.

—CHARLES COLSON

*We must believe
not in ourselves, but in
the greatness of God.*

—UNKNOWN

Oh, how kind and gracious the Lord was!
He filled me completely with faith
and the love of Christ Jesus.

—1 TIMOTHY 1:14, NLT

Faith is the bucket of power lowered by the rope of prayer into the well of God's abundance. What we bring up depends upon what we let down.

—Virginia Whitman

❧

Faith is the strength and courage God gives you to help you to fill each day with words and deeds of love.

—Louisa May Alcott's mother

❧

It is only in believing that we are loved with an everlasting love that we begin to leave our fears behind and experience great joy at the thought of getting to know our Creator better.

—Dr. Deborah Newman

Fear not: for I am with thee.

—Isaiah 43:5, KJV

Be faithful to what God has shown you—and don't worry about what He hasn't. God will reveal to you, in His time, everything you need to know. God wants to foster your dependence on Him. As you learn to love and trust God's faithfulness more, He'll put His peace in your heart.

—Fénelon

Be not perplexed,
Be not afraid,
Everything passes,
God does not change.
Patience wins all things.
He who has God lacks nothing;
God alone suffices.

—Teresa of Avila

God fulfills His promises; our duty is to be faithful.

—Blair Seitz and Ruth Hoover Seitz

I will sing of the Lord's great love forever; with my mouth I will make your faithfulness known through all generations. I will declare that your love stands firm forever, that you established your faithfulness in heaven itself.

—Psalm 89:1-2, niv

Faith is . . .

resting by His side, where the
tranquil waters glide;
Born of Him, through grace renewed,
by His love my will subdued,
Rich in faith I still would be;
let my Savior dwell in me.

—Fanny J. Crosby

Let us with a gladsome mind
Praise the Lord, for He is kind:
For His mercies shall endure.
Ever faithful, ever sure.

—JOHN MILTON

Nobody said life would be perfect. Nobody
said your kids would go through life scot-free
of troubles. But what your kids do need to
know is that God can be trusted to never leave,
no matter how hot the trouble gets. And that's
what you need to know, too, when you're
tempted to jump into your kids' troubles with
both feet—before you get scalded. You're not
the trouble-fixer; God is. And you'd be smart
to remember that!

—BARBARA JOHNSON

PRAYER

"Imagine no heavenly Father listening.
Imagine no outlet for the cries of our hearts.
Imagine life without prayer."

Ron DiCianni

Lord, what a change within us one short hour

   Spent in Thy presence will avail to make!

What heavy burdens from our bosoms take!

   What parched grounds refresh as with a shower!

We kneel, and all around us seem to lower;

   We rise, and all, the distant and the near,

Stands forth in sunny outline, brave and clear;

   We kneel, how weak; we rise, how full of power!

Why, therefore, should we do ourselves this wrong,

   Or others—that we are not always strong—

That we are sometimes overborne with care—

   That we should ever wear or heartless be,

Anxious or troubled—when with us is prayer,

   And joy and strength and courage are with Thee?

—RICHARD C. TRENCH

Q u i e t n e s s

"Be still and know that I am God,"
That I who made and gave thee life
Will lead thy faltering steps aright;
That I who see each sparrow's fall
Will hear and heed thy earnest call.

I am God.

"Be still and know that I am God,"
When aching burdens crush thy heart,
Then know I form thee for thy part
And purpose in the plan I hold.

Trust in God.

"Be still and know that I am God,"
Who made the atom's tiny span
And set it moving to My plan,
That I who guide the stars above
Will guide and keep thee in My love.

Be thou still.

—DORAN

Before they call, I will answer;
and while they are still speaking,
I will hear.

—Isaiah 65:24, NASB

Sweet hour of prayer! sweet hour of prayer!
That calls me from a world of care,
And bids me at my Father's throne
Make all my wants and wishes known.

—William W. Walford

In the midst of everything, mothers should
take time to love and laugh and pray. Then
life will be worth living, each and every day.

—Susan Wall

Oh, the loving strength that surges from his heart to yours all day; like a bright and shining armor, just because you knelt to pray!

—Alice H. Mortenson

If our hearts are listening as we pray, we will from time to time hear, "Why are you praying? Do something!" And we will know what it is that we must do. A wrong to put right, a sin to confess, a letter to write, a friend to visit, or perhaps a child to be rocked and read to.

—Ruth Bell Graham

I pray to you, O Lord. I say, "You are my place of refuge. You are all I really want in life."

—Psalm 142:5, NLT

*A*ll of us—at home, at war, wherever we may be—are within the reach of God's love and power. We all can pray. We all should pray. We should ask the fulfillment of God's will. We should ask for courage, wisdom, for the quietness of soul which comes alone to them who place their lives in his hands.
—HARRY S. TRUMAN

Thank you, dear God,
for all you have given me,
for all you have taken away from me,
for all you have left me!
—UNKNOWN

If you hem in both ends of your day with a prayer, it won't be so likely to unravel in the middle.

—Unknown

A surrendered life was what Mother modeled for us. When life knocked her to her knees, she learned that was the best position for prayer. What a comfort to have a praying mother! She didn't just say prayers—she talked to God! And she talked to Him about our lives, our needs, our future.

—June Hunt

This is my prayer: that your love may abound more and more in knowledge and depth of insight.

—Philippians 1:9, niv

It's easy for us, as humans, to try to figure things out for ourselves, instead of looking to God for what He says. How often do you go directly to God in prayer or to His Word when in the middle of a crisis or situation—before you start worrying? Ask God to help you turn to him first—after all, He's the Master Problem-Solver.

—Josh McDowell

More love to Thee, O Christ,
More love to Thee!
Hear Thou the prayer I make
On bended knee.

—Elizabeth Payson Prentiss

Be glad for all God is planning for you. Be patient in trouble, and always be prayerful.

—Romans 12:12, nlt

Don't be weary in prayer; keep at it; watch for God's answers, and remember to be thankful when they come.

—Colossians 4:2, TLB

Pray much for others; plead for God's mercy upon them; give thanks for all he is going to do for them.

—1 Timothy 2:1, TLB

Prayer is not eloquence, but earnestness; not the definition of helplessness, but the feeling of it; not figures of speech, but earnestness of soul.

—HANNAH MORE

❧

God who sees and provides, thank you for providing us with children to nurture and love. Please help us to notice Your provisions and then to rehearse them with our children, strengthening our faith and encouraging theirs. Amen.

—ELLEN BANKS ELWELL
Quiet Moments of Faith for Moms

❧

He prayeth best who loveth best
All things both great and small;
For the dear God who loveth us
He made and loveth all.

—SAMUEL TAYLOR COLERIDGE

Jesus, Son of human mother,

Bless our motherhood, we pray;

Give us grace to lead our children,

Draw them to thee day by day;

May our sons and daughters

be dedicated, Lord, to thee.

Grant we may thy footsteps follow

Patiently through toil or pain;

May our quiet home-life be lived,

O Lord, in thee, to thee.

—EMILY L. SHIRREFF

A mother's love
  Is a beacon light
That shines faith, and truth, and prayer;
  And through the changing scenes of life,
Her children find a haven there.
—UNKNOWN

I remember my mother's prayers—and they have always followed me. They have clung to me all my life.

—ABRAHAM LINCOLN

We have not stopped praying for you and asking God to fill you with the knowledge of his will through all spiritual wisdom and understanding.

—COLOSSIANS 1:9, NIV

There are no perfect parents, and mine would have been the first to admit their shortcomings. But I have in my mind a lasting picture of my beloved mother kneeling at the side of her bed, a nightly ritual. She taught me that God does not live in a church-shaped box to be visited like a sick relative on Sunday. She showed me a present tense God who would hear my prayers, treat me kindly, and hold me accountable to my parents and to Him at the end of the day.

—Jill Briscoe

Lord,

day by day, year by year,
will you remind us
that through prayer
we have a share
in shaping the world
in our town, on our street?

—RUTH HARMS CALKIN

*E*very day, commit the ones you love
unto God's care and keeping. It's the
best—and the only thing—you can do.

—FAMILY LIFE